I AM A PRESIDENT TOO

By Shanley Simpson

To my greatest creation and biggest inspiration, Summer S.

Copyright © 2022 Shanley Simpson

All rights reserved. No part of this publication may be reproduced, distributed, or transmitted in any form or by any means, including photocopying, recording, or other electronic or mechanical methods, without the prior written permission of the publisher, except in the case of brief quotations embodied in critical reviews and certain other noncommercial uses permitted by copyright law. For permission requests, write to the publisher, addressed "Attention: Permissions Coordinator," at the address below.

This book is not associated, or in partnership, with Kamala Harris or the presidential administration.

ISBNs: Paperback 978-1-63616-105-1
Hardcover 978-1-63616-218-8

Published & Illustarted By
Opportune Independent Publishing Company

Printed in the United States of America

For permission requests, email the publisher with the subject line as "Attention: Permissions Coordinator" to the email address below.

info@opportunepublishing.com
www.opportunepublishing.com

Let me tell you how it all began
with a little girl who
had a big dream and a plan.
When I was a child like you,
I looked around and thought, *What can I do?*
I saw problems and thought, *This isn't fair.*
I knew I could help if I just learned more and cared.

My mom always said, "Speak up my dear,
your voice has power the world needs to hear!"
So, I learned to ask questions,
stand tall and be strong.
I knew in my heart
I could right what was wrong.

I studied hard in school and worked hard every day.
If you want to make changes, there's always a way.
Reading, math, and history too — all the steps to make big dreams come true!

I graduated from college and law school too.
With each diploma, my dreams grew and grew!
I stepped into my career, ready to take my place.
Armed with knowledge and drive, I was prepared for the race.
With each challenge I faced, I grew even more determined
to succeed and keep pace!

One day, I said, "I'll run for office, you'll see!"
I wanted to make laws and help the people in our country.
I became a lawyer and senator too.
Every little step helped my big dreams come true.

People asked, "Kamala, can you really lead?"
I said, "Yes, I can. Just watch me succeed!"
I worked hard, listened and fought for what's right.
I helped people's voices be heard so they could shine bright.

One day, a wonderful thing came true.
I became the Vice President for me and for YOU!

The first of many women, and I'm brown,
showing girls everywhere there's never a need to back down.
When I walk into the White House I smile
because I know every step was worth every mile.
This isn't the end of my story — oh, no!
I have more dreams and places to go.

Even when I'm on TV, laughing and having fun,
I always spread a positive message to everyone.
It's important to share kindness wherever you go.
Your words have power — more than you know!

When you speak with love and light in your heart,
you help others grow strong, thoughtful and smart.

So, whether you're with friends or in the spotlight's gleam,
always share words that are kind and that you truly mean!

If you have a big dream in your heart, stand tall.
Look in the mirror.
And know you're smart after all.

Imagine yourself as president, leading the way.
With hard work and belief, you'll get there someday.

One day, you might be President too,
changing the world with all that you do!
Or maybe a doctor helping others stay well.
Or a teacher with stories and knowledge to tell.
Perhaps a mechanic keeping wheels on the go.
Or a policeman serving and protecting those you know.

So, dream big, work hard and always believe
that you can be and do anything you want to achieve.
With each step you take,
you're building your way
to become who you dream of being one day!

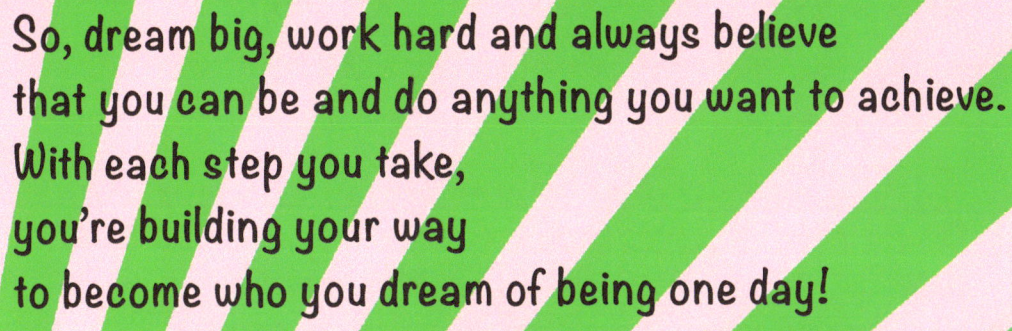

After a hard-fought race,
I became President too.
Leading with care and showing what
big dreaming can do.

No matter where you begin or how big
your dreams may be, work hard and stay
focused, and soon you'll see.
You can achieve absolutely anything, just
like me!

WE LOVE YOU!

www.ingramcontent.com/pod-product-compliance
Lightning Source LLC
Chambersburg PA
CBHW041703160426
43209CB00017B/1733